Placement Test
Intermediate

Harcourt School Publishers

ISBN 10: 0-15-372755-1
ISBN 13: 978-0-15-372755-9

2 3 4 5 6 7 8 9 10   018   12 11 10 09 08

Table of Contents

Placement Test, Intermediate

© Harcourt

Intervention Station
Placement Test, Intermediate

Intervention Station is a program designed to provide teachers with intensive and focused instructional support in the technical skills of reading. The *Placement Test* will help teachers determine which students need the instructional boost provided by *Intervention Station*, and in which of the four major components of the program students need help.

Which students should be administered the test?

The test should be administered to any student who is showing signs of struggling with comprehension and word recognition in the *StoryTown* program. Weekly Lesson Test or Theme Test scores can provide evidence of which students are struggling. However, teacher observations of a student's classroom activities in reading are also very important guidelines. If a student seldom takes part in oral reading of stories or doesn't participate in classroom discussions, the *Placement Test* may be administered to further check on the student's reading skill development. While the *Placement Test* should not be administered routinely to all students, it is a useful tool in identifying a student who may be falling behind.

What reading skills are included on the *Placement Test*?

The major areas of instruction assessed by the *Placement Test* include:

Placement Test, Intermediate

Phonics	30 test items
Comprehension	30 test items
Vocabulary	30 test items
Fluency	80 items plus one passage (all parts are timed)

The *Placement Test* is meant to be a set of diagnostic tests for each of these four instructional areas. The scores will indicate whether or not a student needs the remediation in *Intervention Station* within each skill area. However, each of the four tests is not diagnostic for sub-skills of the major skill area, since the tests only sample from the domain of skills that make up the skill area. For example, the phonics section includes test items for consonants (beginning and ending), short and long vowels, vowel diphthongs, and others. There are not an adequate number of test items to adequately diagnose these phonics skills. However, the phonics test samples from all of these areas and provides a valid and reliable score to determine if the phonics skill area is a problem for the student.

© Harcourt

Should a student be administered all of the test components?

If a student is struggling in daily classroom activities and is not scoring well on Weekly Lesson Tests or Theme Tests in *StoryTown,* it is probably best to administer all four of the tests that comprise the *Placement Test* to determine which area or areas are the most troublesome for the student. However, if a teacher has identified one area that he or she feels is a serious problem area for one or more students, it would be reasonable to administer only that particular reading skill area.

What scores determine placement?

First, each skill area of the test should be scored and the placement score for that area should be determined using the cut scores provided below.

Placement Scores for the *Placement Test, Intermediate* *Intervention Station*

Placement Test, Intermediate				
Placement Decision	Phonics (30 test items)	Comprehension (30 test items)	Vocabulary (30 test items)	Fluency 286*
Low Intervention Station	0 to 14	0 to 14	0 to 14	0 to 139
Medium Possible Intervention Station	15 to 21	15 to 21	15 to 21	140 to 179
High Not Intervention Station	22 to 30	22 to 30	22 to 30	180 to 286

Maximum score is dependent on how many words per minute a student reads.

Placement Test, Intermediate
© Harcourt

How are test results interpreted?

Placement decisions are made using the table.

The primary use of the *Placement Test* is to determine which students can profit from instruction in *Intervention Station*. A student may score low and need intervention in only one skill area or the student may need support in all four technical areas. Note: It is important that teacher judgment based on classroom observation also be used in making all placement decisions. *Scores on the four separate skills tests should be interpreted separately from one another. Each skill area can be interpreted as follows:*

- *Low level performance* indicates a student is definitely in need of focused instruction on that area in *Intervention Station*.

- *Medium level performance* indicates a student may be in need of some instruction in *Intervention Station*. However, teachers should rely on classroom observations by using the program for a limited period of time with these students.

- *High level performance* indicates a student is not in need of focused instruction in *Intervention Station*.

Placement Test, Intermediate

© Harcourt

Score Report
Placement Test, Intermediate
Intervention Station

Write the student's score in the box corresponding to the cut score for each of the four tests.

Student _____ **Date Tested** _____

Test	Possible Score	Placement Decision		
		Low Intervention Station **Placement**	**Medium** **Possible** Intervention Station **Placement**	**High** **Do Not Place in** Intervention Station
Phonics	30	0 to 14	15 to 21	22 to 30
Student's Score		☐	☐	☐
Comprehension	30	0 to 14	15 to 21	22 to 30
Student's Score		☐	☐	☐
Vocabulary	30	0 to 14	15 to 21	22 to 30
Student's Score		☐	☐	☐
Fluency	280	0 to 139	140 to 179	180 to 286
Student's Score		☐	☐	☐

Name _____

▶ **Read each sentence. Each sentence has a blank in it.
Under the sentence are four words. Find the word that
best completes the sentence and fill in the answer circle
next to that word.**

1. Use this _____ to write the note.
   - (A) pin
   - (B) pan
   - (C) pen
   - (D) pun

2. For this game, players need a
   _____ and a ball.
   - (F) bat
   - (G) but
   - (H) bit
   - (I) bet

3. They walked _____ from the
   park.
   - (A) ham
   - (B) hum
   - (C) home
   - (D) him

4. She rides her _____ to school.
   - (F) back
   - (G) bake
   - (H) book
   - (I) bike

5. How _____ can that plane fly?
   - (A) high
   - (B) hide
   - (C) hill
   - (D) had

6. No one _____ what to do next.
   - (F) gnomes
   - (G) notes
   - (H) knows
   - (I) wrists

7. If you're going to be late, you
   should _____ your mom.
   - (A) foam
   - (B) shell
   - (C) then
   - (D) phone

8. We won't let the rain _____
   our picnic.
   - (F) spoil
   - (G) spool
   - (H) spin
   - (I) spoon

Name _____

9. They planted the seeds in the
damp _____.

(A) grind

(B) group

(C) gripe

(D) ground

10. Grandpa grew this lettuce in
his _____.

(F) garter

(G) garden

(H) gentle

(I) garment

11. She used a _____ to pound in
the nails.

(A) handle

(B) hammer

(C) hammock

(D) hurdle

12. Tina corrected the words she
had _____.

(F) misbehaved

(G) informal

(H) untied

(I) misspelled

13. Your _____ comment made the
job easier.

(A) helpless

(B) helpful

(C) useless

(D) harmless

14. It's a good idea to _____
important words and sentences.

(F) subtotal

(G) underline

(H) overpass

(I) undersea

15. Mom warned us not to _____
that rule.

(A) unfair

(B) disappear

(C) disobey

(D) unpack

16. Which _____ painted this
beautiful picture?

(F) artist

(G) breakable

(H) careless

(I) gently

17. Jeff showed us his _____ of sports cards.
- (A) relation
- (B) collection
- (C) conclusion
- (D) action

18. Will you write your name in my _____ book?
- (F) autograph
- (G) obstruction
- (H) invisible
- (I) import

19. Grandma used an old camera to take this _____.
- (A) phonograph
- (B) spectator
- (C) photograph
- (D) biography

20. Our first effort was _____, but we will try again.
- (F) unkindness
- (G) refreshment
- (H) unpleasantly
- (I) unsuccessful

21. Do we have _____ time to finish the project?
- (A) impossible
- (B) expensive
- (C) early
- (D) enough

22. It isn't easy to draw a _____ line.
- (F) caught
- (G) lose
- (H) straight
- (I) learn

23. Don't _____ the hot stove.
- (A) touch
- (B) caught
- (C) tough
- (D) though

24. The runner fell and scraped her _____.
- (F) clear
- (G) care
- (H) covered
- (I) knee

25. We made a _____ card to thank our parents.
- (A) sugar
- (B) sure
- (C) special
- (D) sometimes

26. The _____ reminded everyone
to be quiet.
(F) short
(G) sign
(H) prove
(I) fair

27. Try to _____ how scared we
were!
(A) climbed
(B) clear
(C) children
(D) imagine

28. Because it was so hot, _____ ran
down our faces.
(F) sweat
(G) worry
(H) quite
(I) curve

29. It's a good idea to _____ boots
in rainy weather.
(A) prove
(B) wear
(C) half
(D) care

30. My little brother is too _____ to
go to school.
(F) above
(G) question
(H) young
(I) ago

▶ **Read each passage. Fill in the circle in front of the best answer to each question.**

Big Trouble

Some people keep pet rats. They're tame, friendly, and lots of fun. Wild rats do not make good pets. They can carry disease and spread germs. They squeeze through very small holes and into your house. All they need is a hole the size of a quarter. Once inside, they cause big trouble. They raid your food and spread their germs. They can cause damage by gnawing on wood, plastic, and insulation. They may even chew on electrical wires and cause a fire. If you hear a rat inside your walls, it's time to call a service company to control these pests.

_____

1. What would a service company be expected to do?

   Ⓐ deliver some tame rats

   Ⓑ explain why wild rats are dangerous

   Ⓒ repair any damage

   Ⓓ get rid of the wild rats

2. What is the author's main reason for writing this passage?

   Ⓕ to tell why rats make good pets

   Ⓖ to explain about rats and mice

   Ⓗ to warn you to get rid of wild rats

   Ⓘ to entertain with a funny story about rats

3. Which sentence from the passage includes an opinion?

   Ⓐ They're tame, friendly, and lots of fun.

   Ⓑ They can carry disease and spread germs.

   Ⓒ All they need is a hole the size of a quarter.

   Ⓓ They can cause damage by gnawing on wood, plastic, and insulation.

Daydreamer

Clive had been sitting on the Bulldogs' bench a long time—a really long time. Being second string on defense didn't give him much chance to play. He wasn't paying attention to the game anymore. He was thinking about tomorrow's bike ride with his dad.

Meanwhile, on the field, the Bulldog cornerback had hold of the ball and was running toward the goal line. A daydreaming Clive hadn't noticed! Thaxton Peters had intercepted the ball when the Eagles' quarterback threw a pass. Peters saw where it was headed; and in a sprint, he was at the right place at the right time.

But then one of the Eagles plowed into Peters. He was down, and the ball bounced in a jagged path across the field, where another Eagle fell on it.

"Time out!" called the referee. Peters was helped off the field.

"Get in there, Clive!" the coach ordered. But Clive was still lost in thought.

"Clive! Clive! You want to play or not?" The coach's voice was really loud and forceful. "You're in for Peters."

"Really?" Clive said, squinting at the field. He was trying to figure out what had happened. Suddenly, Clive was going to be playing first-string defense, but he had lost track of the game.

4. What is the main way in which Peters is different from Clive?

(F) Peters is a quarterback; Clive is a cornerback

(G) Peters is on the Eagles' team; Clive is on the Bulldogs' team

(H) Peters ends up in the rest of the game; Clive does not.

(I) Peters is playing in the game; Clive is not.

5. What is the main reason that Coach Harwood puts Clive in the game?

(A) Clive is a good bike rider.

(B) He is tired of watching Clive daydream.

(C) Peters has been injured.

(D) He wants everyone to get to play.

6. What is the author's main reason for writing this passage?

(F) to entertain readers with a sports story

(G) to persuade readers that football is more important than bike riding

(H) to explain how to win a football game

(I) to argue that cornerbacks are more important than quarterbacks

River Dance

Clouds form in the sky. Soon rain begins to fall high in the mountains. It gathers slowly in small pools and finds a crack in a cliff wall. The rainwater rushes through the rocks and finds a trail worn by wild animals. Then it runs downward toward the lowest part of the landscape.

Soon, the stream of water forms a brook. This tiny freshwater rivulet flows into a creek. Other rivulets find their way to the creek. The creek runs down the mountainside and empties into a river. The rainwater is now in the river. It flows over rocks, before falling over cliffs. Down below, the river churns through a canyon, taking soil and rocks with it. At last, the rainwater finds the sea, and the fresh rainwater mixes with salt water in the ocean.

---

7. According to this passage, how does the journey of the rainwater begin?

   (A) It gathers in pools before it rushes through a crack in a cliff.

   (B) Rocks and soil move aside to let a river run through.

   (C) It falls over cliffs.

   (D) Rivulets find their way to a creek.

8. What happens after water flows in a creek?

  (F) Clouds form in the sky.

  (G) Rain falls high in the mountains.

  (H) The creek empties into a river.

  (I) Freshwater mixes with salt water.

9. Which word does NOT help you follow the sequence?

  (A) *slowly*

  (B) *soon*

  (C) *then*

  (D) *at last*

10. What is the main idea in this passage?

  (F) Rain usually starts falling in the mountains.

  (G) Streams of water combine as they travel to the ocean.

  (H) There are many other words for *rainwater*.

  (I) Landforms are created by running water.

The Island

There was only one way off the island—by water. A month had passed, and no one had answered their distress signals. The twelve people stranded on the island would have to save themselves.

Luckily, one of the passengers had helped build a boat before, so he knew what to do. Somsak told the others to choose parts of the shattered plane that they could use to build a raft. He sent them out to find useful things in the jungle. Marta was a great help. As a child, she had learned how to make rope from coconut palm leaves. Anna and Caleb set to work assisting her. Luckily, the plant, with its sword-shaped leaves, grew all over the island. Joe hacked down a tree and hauled its trunk to the beach for a mast. Tran collected a sticky resin from some trees. It would help to waterproof the raft.

Another month passed. Finally, the raft was ready. When, the winds were right, Somsak and two others set sail. On shore, nine others watched the raft drift westward. Hopefully, it would locate a ship or inhabited land soon.

---

11. What is the best conclusion you can draw about this group of people?

   Ⓐ They are on vacation on a tropical island.

   Ⓑ They work for a boat-building company.

   Ⓒ They live in a primitive fishing village.

   Ⓓ They are survivors of a plane crash.

12. Which sentence best represents something the author probably believes?

   Ⓕ If people work together, they can accomplish amazing things.

   Ⓖ Marta is the most valuable person on the island.

   Ⓗ Somsak doesn't need help from the others.

   Ⓘ In times of trouble, your only responsibility is to protect yourself.

13. What is likely to happen if the people on the raft find a ship?

Ⓐ They will go back to the island to live.

Ⓑ They will get the ship to pick up the people on the island.

Ⓒ They will never travel by air again.

Ⓓ They will build more rafts and go back for the others.

14. What is a coconut palm?

Ⓕ a kind of primitive boat

Ⓖ a fire built to send a signal

Ⓗ a rope used in sailing

Ⓘ a kind of tropical plant

15. Which sentence best describes Somsak?

Ⓐ He gives up easily when things get tough.

Ⓑ He is a capable leader who works well with others.

Ⓒ He believes in the old saying "every man for himself."

Ⓓ He is a humble man who is shy when it comes to asking for help.

Newton's First Law of Motion

Have you ever heard of Sir Isaac Newton? Newton was one of the greatest scientists ever to live. He discovered scientific rules, or laws, about movement. We call these laws Newton's Laws of Motion.

Let's find out how Newton's first law of motion works. Newton's first law says this: Objects continue doing what they're doing unless a stronger force acts on them. So, an object that is *not* moving stays at rest. An object that *is* moving keeps moving.

Have you ever watched skateboarders at a skate park? The skaters ride their boards up and down the ramps, making lickity-split turns at the top of each ramp. They go speeding up and down, back and forth, like riders in a Tilt-a-Whirl. What happens if a rider misses the ramp and his board runs into a low barrier? (Let's hope the rider is wearing safety equipment like a helmet and kneepads!) The skateboard stops at the barrier, but the rider keeps going. Why? "Objects continue what they're doing unless a stronger force acts on them." The board hit a stronger force: the barrier. So it stopped. The rider didn't hit anything, so the result was he kept going.

What does the other half of the law say? An object that is not moving stays at rest—unless a stronger force acts on it. Let's assume the skater wasn't hurt. Then how will he get that board moving again? He's going to jump on it and head down the ramp. The stronger force acting on both the skater and the board is gravity. Gravity pulls the board and the skater downhill.

Maybe you didn't know that scientific laws govern the things you do every day. They do, even at the skate park.

16. Which sentence best states the main idea of the passage?

    Ⓕ Newton was one of the greatest scientists ever to live.

    Ⓖ Let's find out how Newton's first law of motion works.

    Ⓗ The skaters ride their boards up and down the ramps, making lickity-split turns at the top of each ramp.

    Ⓘ Let's hope the rider is wearing safety equipment like a helmet and kneepads!

17. According to the passage, what causes a skater to keep going when his board stops?

    Ⓐ the force of gravity

    Ⓑ the Tilt-a-Whirl

    Ⓒ a low barrier

    Ⓓ Newton's first law of motion

18. What is the effect of Newton's first law of motion on an object at rest?

    Ⓕ The law has no effect on a resting object.

    Ⓖ The object stays at rest until a stronger force acts on it.

    Ⓗ The object will start to move without any force acting on it.

    Ⓘ The object will always remain at rest.

19. Which words are clue words that signal a cause-and-effect relationship?

    Ⓐ *back and forth*

    Ⓑ *what happens if*

    Ⓒ *let's assume*

    Ⓓ *how will he get*

20. What two things does the author compare using a simile?

    Ⓕ *skateboarders* and *riders* on *Tilt-a-Whirls*

    Ⓖ *ramps* and *barriers*

    Ⓗ *a helmet* and *kneepads*

    Ⓘ *objects* and *forces*

The Tree House

Claire was younger than her five brothers. She was also the only girl in the family.

Claire was not willing to take a back seat to five boys. By age eight, she was a force to be reckoned with. She was always sure to get her fair share. She did her fair share of the chores, too. She made sure that James, the eldest, set the table and washed the dishes just as often as she did. And the first time Jon and Liam set out to mend the fence around the corral, she made them take her with them. When her mother couldn't figure out how to use her new cell phone, Claire was the one to help her.

But when the boys built a fort down by the creek, Claire was not allowed to help. The boys had done most of it by themselves, but their parents had helped, too.

"It's unfair!" Claire told her parents. "I've wanted a tree house for two years. The boys just came up with their fort idea. Now their fort is done, and nobody's even offered to help me with my tree house!"

"There are five of us," said Charley. "We all wanted a fort."

"Yeah," added Liam. "You're just one person. What are you going to do in a tree house anyway? Read to your dolls?"

Andy, always the quiet one, had been listening to the argument. "Claire has a point," he finally said. "Just because there are five of us, it doesn't mean she shouldn't have what she wants, too—whether she wants to read to dolls or build a time machine up there."

"Yeah, and knowing Claire, she's probably going to build a time machine," said James. The brothers laughed, but they all agreed. Building a tree house for Claire would be their next project.

21. Which sentence best describes Claire?

    (A) She is afraid to try new things.

    (B) She can speak up for herself.

    (C) She is too shy to speak up for herself.

    (D) She has a good sense of humor.

22. What is the setting for this story?

    (F) a ranch

    (G) a fort

    (H) a city

    (I) a tree house

23. What problem arises in the story?

    (A) A girl is born into a family of five older brothers who try to ignore her.

    (B) Claire wants to learn to mend fences, but her parents say it is her brothers' job.

    (C) Five brothers get help with their fort, but Claire needs help to build a tree house.

    (D) Claire wants to build a time machine, but the boys think she should play with dolls.

24. How is the problem solved?

    (F) Jon and Liam take Claire with them to mend fences.

    (G) Mom and Dad help the boys build a fort.

    (H) James helps out by setting the table and washing the dishes.

    (I) The brothers promise to help build a tree house.

The Lion and the Bulls

A Tale from Aesop

Long ago in Africa, a lion roamed the grasslands looking for something to eat. There was plenty of food around. A whole herd of bulls came each day to one particular waterhole. The lion watched them, licking his chops. But each time the lion approached, the bulls formed a ring, facing outward. No matter which way he approached, sharp horns threatened his very life.

On hot days, the bulls waded together in their favorite waterhole. At night, they slept in a group facing outward, like watchful guards on a castle wall. Gazing at them, the lion wasn't sure what he desired more: the cool, sweet water or their tasty flesh.

One day the bulls quarreled. Maybe it was over who was the strongest. Maybe it was about who had the longest horns. Whatever it was, they refused to speak to each other. Each went his separate way to graze where he pleased, and to drink from different pools.

This was the very thing the lion was waiting for. He began pouncing on them from behind. When his belly was full, he drank at leisure from several lovely pools. The silly bulls had forgotten an important truth. The lion, remembering it, went home and lived out the rest of his days.

---

25. Which sentence best states the lesson of this story?

(A) In time of need, the weak may help the strong.

(B) When you try to please everyone, you end up pleasing no one.

(C) You have no right to what is not rightfully yours.

(D) There is safety in numbers.

26. Which sentence best tells what this story is about?

    Ⓕ Many animals can live on a grassland in Africa.

    Ⓖ A herd of bulls outsmarts a hungry lion.

    Ⓗ A lion attacks a quarreling herd of bulls.

    Ⓘ The bulls swam during the day and slept at night.

27. What kind of figurative language is used in this sentence from the story?

At night, they slept in a group facing outward, like watchful guards on a castle wall.

    Ⓐ a simile

    Ⓑ a metaphor

    Ⓒ personification

    Ⓓ hyperbole

28. How did the lion solve his problem?

    Ⓕ He decided not to be afraid of sharp horns.

    Ⓖ He attacked when each bull was alone.

    Ⓗ He tricked the bulls.

    Ⓘ He returned to his pride.

Chichén Itzá

For the first time, ordinary people have chosen the Seven Wonders of the World. People from around the world voted on them by computer. The vote ended on July 7, 2007. Chichén Itzá deserved to become one of the Seven Wonders. And it did.

Chichén Itzá is in eastern Mexico. It covers around four square miles. The ancient site includes some of the world's most amazing buildings. The site's main pyramid is about 78 feet tall, and it is an awesome sight! But there are other amazing buildings at Chichén Itzá. A great meeting hall once had 1,000 columns. The ball court is the largest one ever found in North or Central America. On many ancient walls, you can still see carvings and sculptures.

Archaeologists have done an amazing job putting the ruins back together. There is still a lot to do. So far, only about 20 percent of the buildings have been unearthed. Yet visitors to the site are already amazed. Long ago, Chichén Itzá must have been an amazing place.

___

29. Which statement below is a fact?

Ⓐ Chichén Itzá deserved to become one of the Seven Wonders.

Ⓑ And it is an awesome sight!

Ⓒ The site's main pyramid is about 78 feet tall.

Ⓓ Long ago, Chichén Itzá must have been an amazing place.

30. Which statement below is an opinion?

Ⓕ People from around the world voted on them by computer.

Ⓖ The ancient site includes some of the world's most amazing buildings.

Ⓗ The ball court is the largest one ever found in North or Central America.

Ⓘ So far, only about 20 percent of the buildings have been unearthed.

Name _____

Teacher Read Aloud   Read the Directions,
Test Questions, and Answer Choices to children.

▶ **Fill in the circle in front of the correct answer.**

1. Dad loves to cook and has many _____ tools.

   Ⓐ crooked

   Ⓑ tiresome

   Ⓒ culinary

   Ⓓ dull

2. I would like to see all the beautiful flowers in the park, so Mom said
   we'd take a nice _____ in the morning.

   Ⓕ stroll

   Ⓖ sprint

   Ⓗ nap

   Ⓘ effort

3. Liz was unhappy and _____ at Sparky as he ran through the house
   with muddy paws.

   Ⓐ joked

   Ⓑ smiled

   Ⓒ smirked

   Ⓓ glared

4. Our new science teacher, Mr. Harvey, is very _____ and serious.

   Ⓕ sparkling

   Ⓖ stern

   Ⓗ careless

   Ⓘ vivid

26

© Harcourt •

5. Mother lions can be _____ in order to protect their cubs.

Ⓐ kind

Ⓑ fierce

Ⓒ calm

Ⓓ asleep

6. The car _____ to the side of the road to avoid hitting the deer.

Ⓕ swerved

Ⓖ stopped

Ⓗ jammed

Ⓘ marked

7. "Shh! Class, please sit down and _____ talking!" Mrs. Jameson
said loudly.

Ⓐ begin

Ⓑ alarm

Ⓒ surge

Ⓓ cease

8. It is important for gymnasts and dancers to be _____ so they can
do many acrobatic moves.

Ⓕ serene

Ⓖ flexible

Ⓗ happy

Ⓘ unique

9. The hurt and frightened bird was _____ to its many enemies in the woods.

(A) pliable

(B) superior

(C) vulnerable

(D) unavailable

10. The cheerleaders were quite _____ as they led the huge stadium crowd in the team's fight song.

(F) mellow

(G) exuberant

(H) stubborn

(I) mature

11. What creatures might you find in the _____ of the ocean?

(A) depths

(B) traits

(C) brightness

(D) files

12. For the annual talent show I decided to do a song and _____ my favorite singer.

(F) avoid

(G) contract

(H) release

(I) mimic

13. "This work is _____," Robby moaned, as he finished his
Saturday chores of cutting the grass and raking the leaves.

(A) peculiar

(B) treacherous

(C) drudgery

(D) entertaining

14. Casey prefers bright and colorful clothes to _____ ones.

(F) drab

(G) cold

(H) pristine

(I) long

15. As we entered the museum, we were told that many of the artifacts are very
_____ and we should not touch them.

(A) delectable

(B) seasoned

(C) fragile

(D) fragrant

16. The sun is a _____ star in the center of our solar system.

(F) gifted

(G) brilliant

(H) lifeless

(I) tedious

17. The _____ ballerinas presented *Swan Lake* at the
performing arts center.

    Ⓐ graceful

    Ⓑ vast

    Ⓒ bountiful

    Ⓓ embarrassed

18. Billy loved to bowl, and he _____ that I learn too, so we could
bowl together.

    Ⓕ installed

    Ⓖ confessed

    Ⓗ exposed

    Ⓘ insisted

19. It would only be a matter of time until the _____ clouds dropped
rain on our family picnic.

    Ⓐ gracious

    Ⓑ ominous

    Ⓒ anxious

    Ⓓ hopeful

20. The 1980 United States hockey team's gold medal performance was a _____
accomplishment.

    Ⓕ comfortable

    Ⓖ pathetic

    Ⓗ remarkable

    Ⓘ predictable

21. "I'm afraid I will have to _____ that bad tooth,"
Dr. Brown told Mr. Sanchez.

Ⓐ extract

Ⓑ imitate

Ⓒ fidget

Ⓓ subtract

22. Red, yellow, green, and purple balloons helped make the
room _____ for the party.

Ⓕ disappointing

Ⓖ suspicious

Ⓗ eerie

Ⓘ festive

23. Matthew says that his favorite animals at the zoo are
the _____ elephants.

Ⓐ elegant

Ⓑ petite

Ⓒ massive

Ⓓ embedded

24. "Please fasten your seatbelts while we begin to _____," the
pilot told us.

Ⓕ glisten

Ⓖ endure

Ⓗ verify

Ⓘ descend

25. Dad stopped the car _____ when the traffic light turned red all of a sudden.

Ⓐ abruptly
Ⓑ politely
Ⓒ happily
Ⓓ slowly

26. The neighborhood decided to _____ at city hall to fight the closing of the local park.

Ⓕ compete
Ⓖ protest
Ⓗ cooperate
Ⓘ support

27. Sara's little brother thought the long car ride was very boring and _____.

Ⓐ entertaining
Ⓑ colorful
Ⓒ tolerable
Ⓓ monotonous

28. Supporting your favorite _____ is very important and helps others.

Ⓕ apparel
Ⓖ charity
Ⓗ dwelling
Ⓘ nuisance

29. His friends were _____ after Jay won the state
spelling bee.

(A) ecstatic

(B) practical

(C) careful

(D) dejected

30. Grandpa Jed reminded his grandchildren that it is
a _____ to take a vacation.

(F) disaster

(G) solution

(H) luxury

(I) drawback

33

Assessing Oral Reading Fluency

Assessing oral reading fluency can be done quickly and easily. Have a student read a passage orally while you time the reading and record the reading errors on the Oral Reading Fluency Recording Form.

To administer the oral reading fluency assessment you will need the following:

- a stopwatch or watch with a second hand
- a copy of the passage for the student to read
- a copy of the Recording Form for the same passage for you to mark as the student reads

Once you have selected the passage you will use, follow these steps to conduct the assessment:

1. Explain the task to the student. Tell the student that you want to see how well he or she can read aloud. Inform the student that you will follow along and take notes as he or she reads. The student may ask about the stopwatch and being timed. Encourage the student to read at his or her "normal" pace. You don't want the student to speed up and read artificially fast because of the timing.

2. Have the student begin. Use the stopwatch or second hand to time a one-minute interval as inconspicuously as possible.

3. As the student reads, record reading errors unobtrusively on the Recording Form. Mark mispronunciations, substitutions, omissions of a sound or word, and other errors. *Do not count repetitions, self-corrections, or mispronunciations of proper nouns as reading errors.*

4. When the stopwatch or second hand reaches the one-minute mark, place a slash mark on the Oral Reading Fluency Form after the last word the student reads. Tell the student to stop reading.

Computing the Fluency Score

At the bottom of each Recording Form is a section labeled "Fluency Score." Follow these steps to complete that section and to compute a student's fluency score.

1. Count the total number of words the student read in one or two minutes, depending on directions. The row numbers in the right margin will help you determine the total number quickly. Record this number in the first row, "Total Words Read per 2 Minutes."

2. Count the number of reading errors the student made. Remember: *do not count repetitions or self-corrections as errors.* Record this number in the second row, "Number of Errors."

3. Subtract the number of reading errors (row 2) from the total number of words read (row 1). Record the answer in the third row, "Number of Words Read Correctly." This is the student's oral reading fluency score.

Name _____ Date _____

Oral Reading Fluency Recording Form

▶ **Directions** *This test should take* **two** *minutes to administer.*
Have the child read the words. Start timing when the child
begins reading.

Word Count: 80

lunch	best	stamp	coil	scout	welcome	person	**7**
house	divide	raisin	accepted	dismiss	tough		**13**
wash	above	cool	rest	join	drought	capable	**20**
purple	horrible	interesting	care	tent	volcano		**26**
eastern	trailer	disorder	sweat	myself	loyalty	brown	**33**
spent	suddenly	replay	carpenter	unkind	into	every	**40**
carry	seventy	nickel	plow	forward	action	banana	**47**
knead	uncle	arrow	employ	decided	yellow	upon	**54**
beehive	eagle	crown	weekly	charcoal	mistreat		**60**
biceps	never	because	nation	toil	shout	octopus	**67**
baseball	preset	transport	been	show	likable		**73**
transfer	question	sublet	once	foremost	behave	team	**80**

FLUENCY SCORE

Total Words Read per 2 Minutes   _____

Number of Errors   − _____

Number of Words Read Correctly (WCPM) _____

Placement Test, Intermediate

lunch	best	stamp	coil	scout	welcome	person
house	divide	raisin	accepted	dismiss	tough	
wash	above	cool	rest	join	drought	capable
purple	horrible	interesting	care	tent	volcano	
eastern	trailer	disorder	sweat	myself	loyalty	brown
spent	suddenly	replay	carpenter	unkind	into	every
carry	seventy	nickel	plow	forward	action	banana
knead	uncle	arrow	employ	decided	yellow	upon
beehive	eagle	crown	weekly	charcoal	mistreat	
biceps	never	because	nation	toil	shout	octopus
baseball	preset	transport	been	show	likable	
transfer	question	sublet	once	foremost	behave	team

Placement Test, Intermediate

Oral Reading Fluency Recording Form

▶ **Directions** *This test should take **two** minutes to administer.*
Have the child read the title and the entire passage.
Start timing when the child begins reading.

Word Count: 206

Pecos Bill, Tall Tale Cowboy | 5

The legend is that Bill was born during the 1830s. He	16
was born in Texas, of course. As a baby, he played with	28
bears and wildcats. When Bill was still a baby, his family	39
headed west. They crossed the Pecos River. That's how Bill	49
got his name.	52
One day Bill heard a rattling sound as he walked. He	63
knew a rattlesnake was getting ready to attack. Bill wasn't	73
scared. He even let the snake bite him a few times to show	86
how tough he was. Then Bill just looked mean at that	97
ten-foot rattler. "I give up!" the rattler cried. "No more!	108
Please, Pecos Bill!"	111
Bill had plenty of work to do. He showed ranchers a	122
new way to build fences for a corral. Bill didn't want to	134
do the digging himself. He knew that prairie dogs like to	145
dig holes. He let the little animals dig just so deep. Then	157
he pulled them out. Bill lowered a fence post in each hole.	169
The prairie dogs thought it was fun. Each time they dug a	181
hole, Bill gave them a cookie.	187
At night he sang to them before he went to bed.	198
Their favorite song was "Get Along Little Doggies."	206

FLUENCY SCORE

Total Words Read per 2 Minutes _____

Number of Errors − _____

Number of Words Read Correctly (WCPM) _____

37

Pecos Bill, Tall Tale Cowboy

The legend is that Bill was born during the 1830s. He was born in Texas, of course. As a baby, he played with bears and wildcats. When Bill was still a baby, his family headed west. They crossed the Pecos River. That's how Bill got his name.

One day Bill heard a rattling sound as he walked. He knew a rattlesnake was getting ready to attack. Bill wasn't scared. He even let the snake bite him a few times to show how tough he was. Then Bill just looked mean at that ten-foot rattler. "I give up!" the rattler cried. "No more! Please, Pecos Bill!"

Bill had plenty of work to do. He showed ranchers a new way to build fences for a corral. Bill didn't want to do the digging himself. He knew that prairie dogs like to dig holes. He let the little animals dig just so deep. Then he pulled them out. Bill lowered a fence post in each hole. The prairie dogs thought it was fun. Each time they dug a hole, Bill gave them a cookie.

At night he sang to them before he went to bed. Their favorite song was "Get Along Little Doggies."

Name _____

▶ Read each sentence. Each sentence has a blank in it.
Under the sentence are four words. Find the word that
best completes the sentence and fill in the answer circle
next to that word.

1. Use this _____ to write the note.
   (A) pin
   (B) pan
   (C) pen
   (D) pun

2. For this game, players need a
   _____ and a ball.
   (F) bat
   (G) but
   (H) bit
   (I) bet

3. They walked _____ from the
   park.
   (A) ham
   (B) hum
   (C) home
   (D) him

4. She rides her _____ to school.
   (F) back
   (G) bake
   (H) book
   (I) bike

5. How _____ can that plane fly?
   (A) high
   (B) hide
   (C) hill
   (D) had

6. No one _____ what to do next.
   (F) gnomes
   (G) notes
   (H) knows
   (I) wrists

7. If you're going to be late, you
   should _____ your mom.
   (A) foam
   (B) shell
   (C) then
   (D) phone

8. We won't let the rain _____
   our picnic.
   (F) spoil
   (G) spool
   (H) spin
   (I) spoon

Name _____

9. They planted the seeds in the
   damp _____.
   (A) grind
   (B) group
   (C) gripe
   (D) ground

10. Grandpa grew this lettuce in
    his _____.
    (F) garter
    (G) garden
    (H) gentle
    (I) garment

11. She used a _____ to pound in
    the nails.
    (A) handle
    (B) hammer
    (C) hammock
    (D) hurdle

12. Tina corrected the words she
    had _____.
    (F) misbehaved
    (G) informal
    (H) untied
    (I) misspelled

13. Your _____ comment made the
    job easier.
    (A) helpless
    (B) helpful
    (C) useless
    (D) harmless

14. It's a good idea to _____
    important words and sentences.
    (F) subtotal
    (G) underline
    (H) overpass
    (I) undersea

15. Mom warned us not to _____
    that rule.
    (A) unfair
    (B) disappear
    (C) disobey
    (D) unpack

16. Which _____ painted this
    beautiful picture?
    (F) artist
    (G) breakable
    (H) careless
    (I) gently

Name _____

17. Jeff showed us his _____ of
    sports cards.
    (A) relation
    (B) collection
    (C) conclusion
    (D) action

18. Will you write your name in my
    _____ book?
    (F) autograph
    (G) obstruction
    (H) invisible
    (I) import

19. Grandma used an old camera to
    take this _____.
    (A) phonograph
    (B) spectator
    (C) photograph
    (D) biography

20. Our first effort was _____, but
    we will try again.
    (F) unkindness
    (G) refreshment
    (H) unpleasantly
    (I) unsuccessful

21. Do we have _____ time to finish
    the project?
    (A) impossible
    (B) expensive
    (C) early
    (D) enough

22. It isn't easy to draw a _____ line.
    (F) caught
    (G) lose
    (H) straight
    (I) learn

23. Don't _____ the hot stove.
    (A) touch
    (B) caught
    (C) tough
    (D) though

24. The runner fell and scraped
    her _____.
    (F) clear
    (G) care
    (H) covered
    (I) knee

25. We made a _____ card to thank
    our parents.
    (A) sugar
    (B) sure
    (C) special
    (D) sometimes

Name _____

26. The _____ reminded everyone
    to be quiet.
    (F) short
    (G) sign
    (H) prove
    (I) fair

27. Try to _____ how scared we
    were!
    (A) climbed
    (B) clear
    (C) children
    (D) imagine

28. Because it was so hot, _____ ran
    down our faces.
    (F) sweat
    (G) worry
    (H) quite
    (I) curve

29. It's a good idea to _____ boots
    in rainy weather.
    (A) prove
    (B) wear
    (C) half
    (D) care

30. My little brother is too _____ to
    go to school.
    (F) above
    (G) question
    (H) young
    (I) ago

Placement Test, Intermediate

© Harcourt

▶ Read each passage. Fill in the circle in front of the best
answer to each question.

Big Trouble

Some people keep pet rats. They're tame, friendly, and lots of fun.
Wild rats do not make good pets. They can carry disease and spread
germs. They squeeze through very small holes and into your house.
All they need is a hole the size of a quarter. Once inside, they cause
big trouble. They raid your food and spread their germs. They can cause
damage by gnawing on wood, plastic, and insulation. They may even
chew on electrical wires and cause a fire. If you hear a rat inside your
walls, it's time to call a service company to control these pests.

1. What would a service company be expected to do?
   Ⓐ deliver some tame rats
   Ⓑ explain why wild rats are dangerous
   Ⓒ repair any damage
   Ⓓ get rid of the wild rats

2. What is the author's main reason for writing this passage?
   Ⓕ to tell why rats make good pets
   Ⓖ to explain about rats and mice
   Ⓗ to warn you to get rid of wild rats
   Ⓘ to entertain with a funny story about rats

3. Which sentence from the passage includes an opinion?
   Ⓐ They're tame, friendly, and lots of fun.
   Ⓑ They can carry disease and spread germs.
   Ⓒ All they need is a hole the size of a quarter.
   Ⓓ They can cause damage by gnawing on wood, plastic, and insulation.

Daydreamer

Clive had been sitting on the Bulldogs' bench a long time—a really
long time. Being second string on defense didn't give him much chance to
play. He wasn't paying attention to the game anymore. He was thinking
about tomorrow's bike ride with his dad.

Meanwhile, on the field, the Bulldog cornerback had hold of the ball
and was running toward the goal line. A daydreaming Clive hadn't noticed!
Thaxton Peters had intercepted the ball when the Eagles' quarterback threw
a pass. Peters saw where it was headed; and in a sprint, he was at the right
place at the right time.

But then one of the Eagles plowed into Peters. He was down, and
the ball bounced in a jagged path across the field, where another Eagle
fell on it.

"Time out!" called the referee. Peters was helped off the field.

"Get in there, Clive!" the coach ordered. But Clive was still lost
in thought.

"Clive! Clive! You want to play or not?" The coach's voice was really
loud and forceful. "You're in for Peters."

"Really?" Clive said, squinting at the field. He was trying to figure out
what had happened. Suddenly, Clive was going to be playing first-string
defense, but he had lost track of the game.

4. What is the main way in which Peters is different from Clive?
   Ⓕ Peters is a quarterback; Clive is a cornerback
   Ⓖ Peters is on the Eagles' team; Clive is on the Bulldogs' team
   Ⓗ Peters ends up in the rest of the game; Clive does not.
   Ⓘ Peters is playing in the game; Clive is not.

5. What is the main reason that Coach Harwood puts Clive in
   the game?
   Ⓐ Clive is a good bike rider.
   Ⓑ He is tired of watching Clive daydream.
   Ⓒ Peters has been injured.
   Ⓓ He wants everyone to get to play.

6. What is the author's main reason for writing this passage?
   Ⓕ to entertain readers with a sports story
   Ⓖ to persuade readers that football is more important than bike riding
   Ⓗ to explain how to win a football game
   Ⓘ to argue that cornerbacks are more important than quarterbacks

River Dance

Clouds form in the sky. Soon rain begins to fall high in the mountains.
It gathers slowly in small pools and finds a crack in a cliff wall. The
rainwater rushes through the rocks and finds a trail worn by wild animals.
Then it runs downward toward the lowest part of the landscape.

Soon, the stream of water forms a brook. This tiny freshwater rivulet
flows into a creek. Other rivulets find their way to the creek. The creek
runs down the mountainside and empties into a river. The rainwater is now
in the river. It flows over rocks, before falling over cliffs. Down below, the
river churns through a canyon, taking soil and rocks with it. At last, the
rainwater finds the sea, and the fresh rainwater mixes with salt water in
the ocean.

7. According to this passage, how does the journey of the rainwater begin?
   Ⓐ It gathers in pools before it rushes through a crack in a cliff.
   Ⓑ Rocks and soil move aside to let a river run through.
   Ⓒ It falls over cliffs.
   Ⓓ Rivulets find their way to a creek.

8. What happens after water flows in a creek?

(F) Clouds form in the sky.

(G) Rain falls high in the mountains.

(H) The creek empties into a river.

(I) Freshwater mixes with salt water.

9. Which word does NOT help you follow the sequence?

(A) *slowly*

(B) *soon*

(C) *then*

(D) *at last*

10. What is the main idea in this passage?

(F) Rain usually starts falling in the mountains.

(G) Streams of water combine as they travel to the ocean.

(H) There are many other words for *rainwater*.

(I) Landforms are created by running water.

The Island

There was only one way off the island—by water. A month had passed, and no one had answered their distress signals. The twelve people stranded on the island would have to save themselves.

Luckily, one of the passengers had helped build a boat before, so he knew what to do. Somsak told the others to choose parts of the shattered plane that they could use to build a raft. He sent them out to find useful things in the jungle. Marta was a great help. As a child, she had learned how to make rope from coconut palm leaves. Anna and Caleb set to work assisting her. Luckily, the plant, with its sword-shaped leaves, grew all over the island. Joe hacked down a tree and hauled its trunk to the beach for a mast. Tran collected a sticky resin from some trees. It would help to waterproof the raft.

Another month passed. Finally, the raft was ready. When, the winds were right, Somsak and two others set sail. On shore, nine others watched the raft drift westward. Hopefully, it would locate a ship or inhabited land soon.

11. What is the best conclusion you can draw about this group
of people?

(A) They are on vacation on a tropical island.

(B) They work for a boat-building company.

(C) They live in a primitive fishing village.

(D) They are survivors of a plane crash.

12. Which sentence best represents something the author probably believes?

(F) If people work together, they can accomplish amazing things.

(G) Marta is the most valuable person on the island.

(H) Somsak doesn't need help from the others.

(I) In times of trouble, your only responsibility is to protect yourself.

13. What is likely to happen if the people on the raft find a ship?

(A) They will go back to the island to live.

(B) They will get the ship to pick up the people on the island.

(C) They will never travel by air again.

(D) They will build more rafts and go back for the others.

14. What is a coconut palm?

(F) a kind of primitive boat

(G) a fire built to send a signal

(H) a rope used in sailing

(I) a kind of tropical plant

15. Which sentence best describes Somsak?

(A) He gives up easily when things get tough.

(B) He is a capable leader who works well with others.

(C) He believes in the old saying "every man for himself."

(D) He is a humble man who is shy when it comes to asking for help.

Newton's First Law of Motion

Have you ever heard of Sir Isaac Newton? Newton was one of the greatest scientists ever to live. He discovered scientific rules, or laws, about movement. We call these laws Newton's Laws of Motion.

Let's find out how Newton's first law of motion works. Newton's first law says this: Objects continue doing what they're doing unless a stronger force acts on them. So, an object that is *not* moving stays at rest. An object that *is* moving keeps moving.

Have you ever watched skateboarders at a skate park? The skaters ride their boards up and down the ramps, making lickity-split turns at the top of each ramp. They go speeding up and down, back and forth, like riders in a Tilt-a-Whirl. What happens if a rider misses the ramp and his board runs into a low barrier? (Let's hope the rider is wearing safety equipment like a helmet and kneepads!) The skateboard stops at the barrier, but the rider keeps going. Why? "Objects continue what they're doing unless a stronger force acts on them." The board hit a stronger force: the barrier. So it stopped. The rider didn't hit anything, so the result was he kept going.

What does the other half of the law say? An object that is not moving stays at rest—unless a stronger force acts on it. Let's assume the skater wasn't hurt. Then how will he get that board moving again? He's going to jump on it and head down the ramp. The stronger force acting on both the skater and the board is gravity. Gravity pulls the board and the skater downhill.

Maybe you didn't know that scientific laws govern the things you do every day. They do, even at the skate park.

16. Which sentence best states the main idea of the passage?

(F) Newton was one of the greatest scientists ever to live.

(G) Let's find out how Newton's first law of motion works.

(H) The skaters ride their boards up and down the ramps, making lickity-split turns at the top of each ramp.

(I) Let's hope the rider is wearing safety equipment like a helmet and kneepads!

17. According to the passage, what causes a skater to keep going when his board stops?

(A) the force of gravity

(B) the Tilt-a-Whirl

(C) a low barrier

(D) Newton's first law of motion

18. What is the effect of Newton's first law of motion on an object at rest?

(F) The law has no effect on a resting object.

(G) The object stays at rest until a stronger force acts on it.

(H) The object will start to move without any force acting on it.

(I) The object will always remain at rest.

19. Which words are clue words that signal a cause-and-effect relationship?

(A) *back and forth*

(B) *what happens if*

(C) *let's assume*

(D) *how will he get*

20. What two things does the author compare using a simile?

(F) *skateboarders* and *riders on Tilt-a-Whirls*

(G) *ramps* and *barriers*

(H) *a helmet* and *kneepads*

(I) *objects* and *forces*

20

The Tree House

Claire was younger than her five brothers. She was also the only girl in the family.

Claire was not willing to take a back seat to five boys. By age eight, she was a force to be reckoned with. She was always sure to get her fair share. She did her fair share of the chores, too. She made sure that James, the eldest, set the table and washed the dishes just as often as she did. And the first time Jon and Liam set out to mend the fence around the corral, she made them take her with them. When her mother couldn't figure out how to use her new cell phone, Claire was the one to help her.

But when the boys built a fort down by the creek, Claire was not allowed to help. The boys had done most of it by themselves, but their parents had helped, too.

"It's unfair!" Claire told her parents. "I've wanted a tree house for two years. The boys just came up with their fort idea. Now their fort is done, and nobody's even offered to help me with my tree house!"

"There are five of us," said Charley. "We all wanted a fort."

"Yeah," added Liam. "You're just one person. What are you going to do in a tree house anyway? Read to your dolls?"

Andy, always the quiet one, had been listening to the argument. "Claire has a point," he finally said. "Just because there are five of us, it doesn't mean she shouldn't have what she wants, too—whether she wants to read to dolls or build a time machine up there."

"Yeah, and knowing Claire, she's probably going to build a time machine," said James. The brothers laughed, but they all agreed. Building a tree house for Claire would be their next project.

21

---

21. Which sentence best describes Claire?

(A) She is afraid to try new things.

(B) She can speak up for herself.

(C) She is too shy to speak up for herself.

(D) She has a good sense of humor.

22. What is the setting for this story?

(F) a ranch

(G) a fort

(H) a city

(I) a tree house

23. What problem arises in the story?

(A) A girl is born into a family of five older brothers who try to ignore her.

(B) Claire wants to learn to mend fences, but her parents say it is her brothers' job.

(C) Five brothers get help with their fort, but Claire needs help to build a tree house.

(D) Claire wants to build a time machine, but the boys think she should play with dolls.

24. How is the problem solved?

(F) Jon and Liam take Claire with them to mend fences.

(G) Mom and Dad help the boys build a fort.

(H) James helps out by setting the table and washing the dishes.

(I) The brothers promise to help build a tree house.

22

The Lion and the Bulls

A Tale from Aesop

Long ago in Africa, a lion roamed the grasslands looking for something to eat. There was plenty of food around. A whole herd of bulls came each day to one particular waterhole. The lion watched them, licking his chops. But each time the lion approached, the bulls formed a ring, facing outward. No matter which way he approached, sharp horns threatened his very life.

On hot days, the bulls waded together in their favorite waterhole. At night, they slept in a group facing outward, like watchful guards on a castle wall. Gazing at them, the lion wasn't sure what he desired more: the cool, sweet water or their tasty flesh.

One day the bulls quarreled. Maybe it was over who was the strongest. Maybe it was about who had the longest horns. Whatever it was, they refused to speak to each other. Each went his separate way to graze where he pleased, and to drink from different pools.

This was the very thing the lion was waiting for. He began pouncing on them from behind. When his belly was full, he drank at leisure from several lovely pools. The silly bulls had forgotten an important truth. The lion, remembering it, went home and lived out the rest of his days.

---

25. Which sentence best states the lesson of this story?

(A) In time of need, the weak may help the strong.

(B) When you try to please everyone, you end up pleasing no one.

(C) You have no right to what is not rightfully yours.

(D) There is safety in numbers.

23

26. Which sentence best tells what this story is about?

    F Many animals can live on a grassland in Africa.

    G A herd of bulls outsmarts a hungry lion.

    H A lion attacks a quarreling herd of bulls.

    I The bulls swam during the day and slept at night.

27. What kind of figurative language is used in this sentence from the story?

    At night, they slept in a group facing outward, like watchful guards on a castle wall.

    A a simile

    B a metaphor

    C personification

    D hyperbole

28. How did the lion solve his problem?

    F He decided not to be afraid of sharp horns.

    G He attacked when each bull was alone.

    H He tricked the bulls.

    I He returned to his pride.

Chichén Itzá

For the first time, ordinary people have chosen the Seven Wonders of the World. People from around the world voted on them by computer. The vote ended on July 7, 2007. Chichén Itzá deserved to become one of the Seven Wonders. And it did.

Chichén Itzá is in eastern Mexico. It covers around four square miles. The ancient site includes some of the world's most amazing buildings. The site's main pyramid is about 78 feet tall, and it is an awesome sight! But there are other amazing buildings at Chichén Itzá. A great meeting hall once had 1,000 columns. The ball court is the largest one ever found in North or Central America. On many ancient walls, you can still see carvings and sculptures.

Archaeologists have done an amazing job putting the ruins back together. There is still a lot to do. So far, only about 20 percent of the buildings have been unearthed. Yet visitors to the site are already amazed. Long ago, Chichén Itzá must have been an amazing place.

_____

29. Which statement below is a fact?

    A Chichén Itzá deserved to become one of the Seven Wonders.

    B And it is an awesome sight!

    C The site's main pyramid is about 78 feet tall.

    D Long ago, Chichén Itzá must have been an amazing place.

30. Which statement below is an opinion?

    F People from around the world voted on them by computer.

    G The ancient site includes some of the world's most amazing buildings.

    H The ball court is the largest one ever found in North or Central America.

    I So far, only about 20 percent of the buildings have been unearthed.

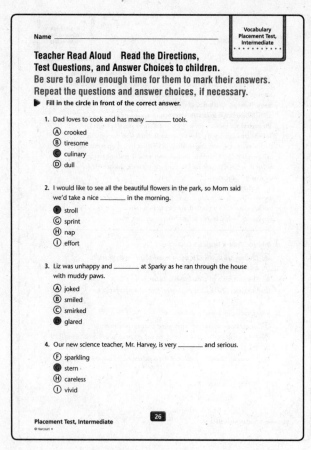

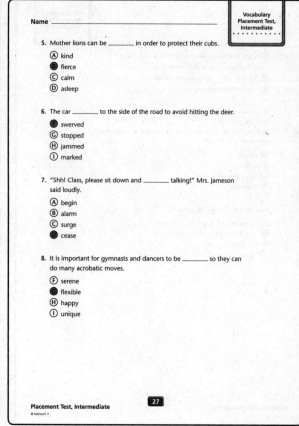

Name _____

**Teacher Read Aloud   Read the Directions,
Test Questions, and Answer Choices to children.**
Be sure to allow enough time for them to mark their answers.
Repeat the questions and answer choices, if necessary.

▶ Fill in the circle in front of the correct answer.

1. Dad loves to cook and has many _____ tools.
   - (A) crooked
   - (B) tiresome
   - (C) culinary
   - (D) dull

2. I would like to see all the beautiful flowers in the park, so Mom said we'd take a nice _____ in the morning.
   - (F) stroll
   - (G) sprint
   - (H) nap
   - (I) effort

3. Liz was unhappy and _____ at Sparky as he ran through the house with muddy paws.
   - (A) joked
   - (B) smiled
   - (C) smirked
   - (D) glared

4. Our new science teacher, Mr. Harvey, is very _____ and serious.
   - (F) sparkling
   - (G) stern
   - (H) careless
   - (I) vivid

Name _____

5. Mother lions can be _____ in order to protect their cubs.
   - (A) kind
   - (B) fierce
   - (C) calm
   - (D) asleep

6. The car _____ to the side of the road to avoid hitting the deer.
   - (F) swerved
   - (G) stopped
   - (H) jammed
   - (I) marked

7. "Shh! Class, please sit down and _____ talking!" Mrs. Jameson said loudly.
   - (A) begin
   - (B) alarm
   - (C) surge
   - (D) cease

8. It is important for gymnasts and dancers to be _____ so they can do many acrobatic moves.
   - (F) serene
   - (G) flexible
   - (H) happy
   - (I) unique

Name _____

9. The hurt and frightened bird was _____ to its many enemies in the woods.
   - (A) pliable
   - (B) superior
   - (C) vulnerable
   - (D) unavailable

10. The cheerleaders were quite _____ as they led the huge stadium crowd in the team's fight song.
    - (F) mellow
    - (G) exuberant
    - (H) stubborn
    - (I) mature

11. What creatures might you find in the _____ of the ocean?
    - (A) depths
    - (B) traits
    - (C) brightness
    - (D) files

12. For the annual talent show I decided to do a song and _____ my favorite singer.
    - (F) avoid
    - (G) contract
    - (H) release
    - (I) mimic

Name _____

13. "This work is _____," Robby moaned, as he finished his Saturday chores of cutting the grass and raking the leaves.
    - (A) peculiar
    - (B) treacherous
    - (C) drudgery
    - (D) entertaining

14. Casey prefers bright and colorful clothes to _____ ones.
    - (F) drab
    - (G) cold
    - (H) pristine
    - (I) long

15. As we entered the museum, we were told that many of the artifacts are very _____ and we should not touch them.
    - (A) delectable
    - (B) seasoned
    - (C) fragile
    - (D) fragrant

16. The sun is a _____ star in the center of our solar system.
    - (F) gifted
    - (G) brilliant
    - (H) lifeless
    - (I) tedious

17. The _____ ballerinas presented *Swan Lake* at the
performing arts center.
   Ⓐ graceful
   Ⓑ vast
   Ⓒ bountiful
   Ⓓ embarrassed

18. Billy loved to bowl, and he _____ that I learn too, so we could
bowl together.
   Ⓕ installed
   Ⓖ confessed
   Ⓗ exposed
   Ⓘ insisted

19. It would only be a matter of time until the _____ clouds dropped
rain on our family picnic.
   Ⓐ gracious
   Ⓑ ominous
   Ⓒ anxious
   Ⓓ hopeful

20. The 1980 United States hockey team's gold medal performance was a _____
accomplishment.
   Ⓕ comfortable
   Ⓖ pathetic
   Ⓗ remarkable
   Ⓘ predictable

21. "I'm afraid I will have to _____ that bad tooth,"
Dr. Brown told Mr. Sanchez.
   Ⓐ extract
   Ⓑ imitate
   Ⓒ fidget
   Ⓓ subtract

22. Red, yellow, green, and purple balloons helped make the
room _____ for the party.
   Ⓕ disappointing
   Ⓖ suspicious
   Ⓗ eerie
   Ⓘ festive

23. Matthew says that his favorite animals at the zoo are
the _____ elephants.
   Ⓐ elegant
   Ⓑ petite
   Ⓒ massive
   Ⓓ embedded

24. "Please fasten your seatbelts while we begin to _____," the
pilot told us.
   Ⓕ glisten
   Ⓖ endure
   Ⓗ verify
   Ⓘ descend

25. Dad stopped the car _____ when the traffic light
turned red all of a sudden.
   Ⓐ abruptly
   Ⓑ politely
   Ⓒ happily
   Ⓓ slowly

26. The neighborhood decided to _____ at city hall to fight the
closing of the local park.
   Ⓕ compete
   Ⓖ protest
   Ⓗ cooperate
   Ⓘ support

27. Sara's little brother thought the long car ride was very
boring and _____.
   Ⓐ entertaining
   Ⓑ colorful
   Ⓒ tolerable
   Ⓓ monotonous

28. Supporting your favorite _____ is very important and
helps others.
   Ⓕ apparel
   Ⓖ charity
   Ⓗ dwelling
   Ⓘ nuisance

29. His friends were _____ after Jay won the state
spelling bee.
   Ⓐ ecstatic
   Ⓑ practical
   Ⓒ careful
   Ⓓ dejected

30. Grandpa Jed reminded his grandchildren that it is
a _____ to take a vacation.
   Ⓕ disaster
   Ⓖ solution
   Ⓗ luxury
   Ⓘ drawback